Published by Experience Transfer, LLC



ISBN : 978-0-9712883-2-4

Revision History
Rev 1. May 2012
Rev 2. March 2013

Piracy

We have agreed to exchange a small amount of money for one copy of this book. If is our belief that honorable people will continue to support this even-exchange agreement. We take unauthorized duplication seriously whether electronic or physical. Emailing to others and posting online are forms of electronic copying. Unauthorized duplication is illegal. If you need multiple copies, we have aggressive bulk purchase pricing and licensing in order to work WITH you.

IBM Trademarks

Cognos and Report Studio are trademarks of IBM.

Bulk purchasing

Contact us for bulk purchasing and reproduction licensing.

INTRODUCTION....4

YOU MUST KNOW YOUR DATA....7

What You Need to Understand about your Data....7

REPORT FRAME CAN ONLY BE POPULATED FROM A SINGLE QUERY....9

NO ITERATION....11

Some approaches to solving iteration challenges:....11

NO GLOBAL VALUES....14

Global Variables in Report Studio....15

NO COMPLEX ROW-TO-ROW CALCULATIONS....17

Possible work around to row-by-row calculations....19

FORMATTING IS A SLIPPERY SLOPE....20

Major challenges in formatting....20

SOME COMPLEX LOGIC IS BEST DONE IN A STORED PROCEDURE OR FUNCTION....24

MULTIPLE WAYS....26

REPORT MUST BE MADE FROM A SINGLE PACKAGE ONLY*....28

How to get around the one package per report limitation.....28

REPORT STUDIO WILL NOT INVENT DATA FOR YOU....30

How to solve the missing data problem....30

CONCLUSION....34

SERVICES AND PRODUCTS....37

Cognos Training....37

JavaScript Report Enhancement....37

Consulting....38

Other Booklets....38

# Introduction

This booklet is written for someone who is about to learn or who has a working knowledge of Report Studio but feels there is much more to learn. It's for beginning through intermediate Report Studio Developers.

If you reflect on other learning you have done, you probably followed a sequence of first learning how to do things. After many months, false starts, lost hours, and under-potential outcomes, you start to learn about the right way to approach a problem, you gain a deeper understanding about the strengths and weaknesses of your previous attempts, and in short, you learn at a much deeper level. Once you get more experience, you begin to really know how to be productive, when one approach is better than another, where the dead ends are and other truly valuable knowledge.

Behind all knowledge with any software system, language or other technology are unwritten guiding principles. This booklet contains 10 principles which will create a framework for all of your report development using Report Studio.

Principles are summarized knowledge, not specific techniques. I find that memorizing in technology is not the way to go due to the rapid rate of change. I do however find great value in memorizing principles as they change much slower and last through many versions or paradigms.

It is my hope that the information contained here will save you months of learning the hard way, make you a better developer after one reading, help you make better performing, more maintainable reports and continue to add value as you move to a much higher level of understanding how Report Studio should be used. Subsequent reads or even individual subjects will continue to evolve you.

It is my experience that books and information like that which is contained within this booklet is fairly rare. I have lived a 30 year life as a PC developer and bought thousands of dollars of technical books, read thousands of web postings, am a very proficient web searcher and am able to digest information fairly quickly. This type of knowledge is fairly rare. You will occasionally find it as an off-hand remark in a technical book, but rarely as its' own paragraph let alone chapter.

I believe that this occurs for four reasons:

1) At the deepest levels of knowledge, any skills become unconscious ... people know what to do but are not really sure exactly why and putting words to the reasons becomes very difficult. See: http://en.wikipedia.org/wiki/Four_stages_of_competence

2) Technical people are generally known for not being able to communicate about technology in non-technical ways and thus create a learning barrier to those without a significant technical understanding and vocabulary. Translating from highly complex into simple is very difficult.

3) Most people cannot summarize knowledge into essential principles or overarching rules.

4) Some people feel that this hard-won knowledge is too valuable to share and would create competition and comparison for themselves.

This booklet will however teach you some of the more difficult things to learn about Report Studio. The underlying rules or principles that are often not conveyed by traditional books and training. The art of using Report Studio as contrasted to the technique.

For illustration of what this booklet is, we are referring to the difference between knowing how to use a word processing program, and knowing how to write clear, simple sentences into paragraphs and paragraphs into chapters.

Learning how to work the word processor takes a few weeks. Learning to write clearly and simply takes years.

This booklet hopes to accelerate your experience by many months and to help you become an advanced developer in ½ the time. Read the information and observe the principles in action as you develop reports. When you get stuck on developing a report, come here and reread the sections and it may trigger ideas. Eventually, this knowledge will become part of you and sink into the unconscious and guide your work in an ongoing way. It is my sincere hope that I can help you get there significantly faster than you normally would have.

Let me know where I succeed and fail. I'm a Kaizen writer.

Ray Hogan
Branchburg, NJ

# You Must Know Your Data

Don't listen to the marketing hype. You cannot ever build a meaningful report by merely knowing how to use any report building tool. Crucially, you also need to understand your data.

Typically, it takes months of regular work to gain the level of understanding of the underlying data in order to have the background to create higher-level, meaningful reports.

By understanding your data I mean many different things.

## What You Need to Understand about your Data

- You need to understand not only the name of different data elements, but also the meaning or definition of each data element, what it is and is not. This is commonly not understood by non-reporting people. I've seen very experienced IT people not understand this point.

- You need to understand reasonable and expected values and ranges of values.

- You need to understand whether or not blanks or nulls are allowed, and where.

- You need to understand the interrelationships between tables... if there is a relationship at all, a one to one, one-to-many or many-to-many relationship, can I have none instead of one or must I have at least one? This needs to be known for the entire database or at least the parts on which you are reporting. You need to understand which values are required and which ones are not.

- You also have to understand the contents of the data as a set. In many cases, the data you are reporting on will come from a software system that has evolved over time and the data may reflect those discrepancies and you will have holes and different subsets of data based on what period of time your report covers.

- You need to understand how the data changes and has changed over time. Are old records static, or are edits constantly made to them, how many new records are added each day? Is old data removed?

- You need to understand whether or not you are reporting from a live database (the one used for the application) or, are you using a database where the data is copied for reporting purposes. If it is copied, what is the frequency of the copy and when does it occur?

- You need to understand how the quality of the data is protected. It is very common to find problems in the data. For example, you may find that states are listed in the wrong country, names of products are spelled different ways, negative numbers exist where only positive ones should and a host of other "dirty data".

- Another common problem is when there is a software system without the best data controls, and you, as the person pulling the data back out for reporting come across "bad data". The data could be inconsistently entered, could have meaningless combinations, typographical errors, transcription problems and much more.

In order to make a report, you need to know much more than which fields to include, you must know your data and its qualities and characteristics. Only then can you make a meaningful, accurate or at least a properly disclosed report that can bring value to an organization.

# Report Frame Can Only be Populated from a Single Query

In Report Studio, there is an absolute limitation that you need to understand as it has a significant impact on your query and layout design.

A "Report Frame" or "Report Object" in Report Studio is a single list, crosstab, chart, repeater, map or other reporting mechanism. In Report Studio, you can have many different report frames on one page, or spread across multiple pages. With master-detail reports, you can even have one frame inside of a list frame.

If you look into the properties of any one of the report frames, you will see that only one query can be specified. This is an absolute limitation in Report Studio that you need to understand as it has a significant impact on your approach to fulfilling reporting requirements.

This "one query per frame" limitation causes you to devise report techniques including query strategies and layout techniques that will impact how you develop reports.

To be more specific, I am saying that if you have very complex requirements for a single report frame, you need to get all of the data into one final query. This is done through advanced query techniques including joins, unions, calculations and filters.

In a large sense, the process of getting your data into one query is the primary task of the advanced report developer and, you will normally spend significant time on implementing your query strategy in order to reach that final query.

Some people will sometimes attempt to fulfill reporting requirements by putting multiple list frames next to each other or on top of each other. This can sometimes be done but a multitude of formatting problems will typically be encountered causing the developer to abandon their attempt to solve the problem in this way. The preferred approach is to spend design time in structuring a final single query that gets the data into a reportable format, and then attaching that single query to a single report frame.

# No Iteration

If you are not deeply experienced in SQL and the strategies involved with working with sets of data, you may come to report development with an assumption that you can get a set of data, perform a "step through" of the data applying logic or calculations, and then show your data in the body of a report. Programmers call stepping through a set of data “Iteration”.

Unfortunately, there is no ability to step through a set of data (result set) in Cognos.

Instead, as a Cognos report developer, your thinking needs to change to devising ways to solve your data challenges within the query... typically by the database server.

## Some approaches to solving iteration challenges:

### Solutions within Report Studio

#### Query Strategy

Probably 80% of your tricky reporting requirements can be solved using queries in creative ways. You may need to do various transformations and calculations, use different kinds of joins and unions, use summary functions and invent data, but a majority of the time, you will be able to solve your data manipulation challenges using Queries

#### Summary Functions

If you don't know about summary functions, take some time and learn them. Summary functions can perform aggregation functions of sub-groups of your data. Things like Total, Minimum, count, average, standard deviation, running-count and many others are built into Report Studio. Using these in conjunction with query strategy or even nesting summary functions can sometimes solve iteration problems. You can find summary functions when in an expression box under the functions tab ... look for "summary". My Companion booklet covers the use and syntax of summary functions.

## Solutions Outside of Cognos

When going outside a packaged solution like Cognos, you will often run into various organizational limitations and delays. You may find that it takes weeks or months and lots of arm twisting to be able to implement the solutions below. It's part of large organization life that these "people challenges" exist and need to be overcome as part of your technical challenge.

### User Defined functions

Sometimes, you can solve your query challenges by adding a database-side function at a crucial point and then use the function within your queries. This function needs to be added to your package by your modeler for you to have access to it in Report Studio.

### Stored Procedures

There are logical conditions that may call for more programmatic control (looping, decision making, jumping around your data, calculations) in order to properly process the data, and a stored procedure should have all of the capabilities that you need to get this done. Once someone writes the stored procedure, the modeler can model the output of the Stored Procedure and make it available for your reporting.

### ETL Table Preparation

Another approach that is sometimes the right one is to prepare the data according to your reporting requirement as part of the data preparation process... commonly referred to as ETL. (Extract-Transform-Load). Similar to stored procedures, you can apply any type of logic and calculations to your data.

However, in this case, the data is actually stored in its final state so the report would be much faster as the processing is done in advance by the ETL process.

Getting around not having iteration in Cognos is mostly a mindset change and you will find that the majority of the time, with some technical creativity, you can overcome this SQL imposed limitation.

# No Global Values

In IT development, there is a concept known of as a global variable. A global variable is a mechanism that allows a developer to specify some data value that needs to be used universally throughout an application. The other reason it is used is for managing relatively consistent piece of information you know will change or has a chance of changing.

A good conceptual example is something like a copyright notice at the bottom of a website. If you were a web developer you could choose between adding the copyright at the bottom of each page, or, put in a reference to another file that contains the copyright information. The benefit of the reference is that when the year changes, you would need to only change one file, not every page in your website. (This is more generally known as an include file, but the concept of centralizing change is the same as with Global Values)

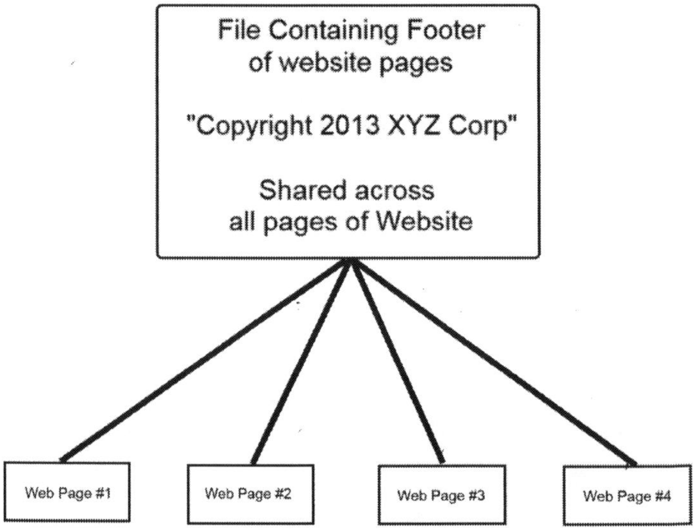

Many years ago, towards the beginning of the web, I worked with someone from a major standards organization. They had created 80,000 web pages and now found themselves needing to change something in all of their pages that would have easily been handled using the global value approach (in this case, referred to as an include file). Unfortunately, they had not entered them into the 80,000 pages originally and therefore had to edit every page inserting the code that enabled the include file (global variable) solution. After that multi-month, multi employee and expensive effort, they were proponents of the global variable approach.

Another example is if you owned a web-based solution (application) and sold it to different customers. As the owner, you probably would want to be able to quickly change the branding and naming of the application when you sold the application to another customer. If you had used a global variable approach in your original design, making these changes would be trivial.

## Global Variables in Report Studio

Unfortunately in Report Studio there is no concept of a global variable. Sometimes in report development, you may want to have a value used throughout a report. Say you need to have many calculations within the report use a standard factor, but over time, that factor will change. You could place the factor in all of the calculations individually, or look to use some type of global variable solution. There is a way to achieve the same effect, but if you have grown used to having global variables elsewhere, without this technique you may feel a small setback when developing in Report Studio. In report Studio, you can share design (non functional) parts of reports, and you can share appearance settings (CSS) across reports, but there is no global variable for controlling the internal functioning of the reports.

In Report Studio, you can solve the problems normally solved by a global variable by using a hidden prompt where the static choice is set (and therefore carried around in the parameter). You then use the parameter as you would a global variable. You hide the prompt by setting its visible property to "no".

# No Complex Row-To-Row Calculations

When you add a basic calculation in Report Studio, it is very common to take the value in one column and use it in combination with another column to produce a new column. For example: determining the unit price if it was not stored in the database as shown below. All calculations like this imply the values all come from the same row. (Here the per-unit calculation divides total price by units purchased).

## Base Data

| Customer | Month | Units purchased | Total Price |
|---|---|---|---|
| Jones | June | 14 | 2912 |
| Jones | July | 7 | 1785 |
| Jones | August | 9 | 2385 |

## Per Unit Price Calculation

| Customer | Month | Units purchased | Total Price | Per Unit |
|---|---|---|---|---|
| Jones | June | 14 | 2912 | 208 |
| Jones | July | 7 | 1785 | 255 |
| Jones | August | 9 | 2385 | 265 |

By far, this type of calculation is what you will perform and Report Studio handles this with not much more than some basic arithmetical syntax.

However, sometimes in report development, you may come across the need to perform a calculation in the current row based on or including the value in a previous row or several rows away.

For example, here I am showing the difference between the first row and the second row's total price.

## Cross Row Calculation (Running-difference)

| Customer | Month | Units purchased | Total Price | Per Unit | M-T-M Diff |
|---|---|---|---|---|---|
| Jones | June | 14 | 2912 | 208 | |
| Jones | July | 7 | 1785 | 255 | -1127 |
| Jones | August | 9 | 2385 | 265 | 600 |

Using summary functions, you can perform the most basic row-to-row calculations (running-total and running-difference). However, if you want to do something beyond that, it gets more and more complex and quickly reaches the impossible (or severely impractical).

For example, you may want to know the difference from a few rows ago, or, you may want to use some logic that first checks a value a few rows ago and then applies a different calculation based on that value.

Report Studio, and SQL for that matter widely support “within row” calculations. Doing cross-row calculations beyond the most basic ones are possible but only using extremely complex query strategies.

# Possible work around to row-by-row calculations

It is theoretically possible to do a more complex row-to row-calculation in Report Studio by creating two queries and joining them based on an invented key value in both queries that are offset, allowing you to put two different rows' values all on the same row as a result of the join. Here, you are still only doing within row calculations but the join allows you to place different rows values within the same row.

However, once you get the offset row join working there are then first and last row challenges to contend with.

All of these computational complications can be overcome, but you may be better served performing the row to row work in a stored procedure, function, or in your ETL or elsewhere as the logic and programmatic mobility within the set of rows is much more direct and easier to work with.

In summary, as a general rule, I recommend you have a mental trigger that should alert you to a row-to-row calculation or logical situation and look long and hard at the exact details of that calculation. There is a good possibility that solving it may require you to have work done outside of Cognos in order to fulfill the requirement and this may affect your time estimates.

# Formatting is a Slippery Slope

In all I.T. development, whenever you deliver something to an end user, you have an additional concern of usability and understandability.

Issues like good labeling, menu choice names and organization, font size and color, flow, layout positioning for ease of locating, pleasing color schemes and more. In fact, user interface design is a discipline and a career path in IT. Perhaps 10-30% of your report development time can be spent in formatting... more if your reports reach a high level audience.

You should always keep an eye on the time you spend on developing a report in regards to the look and feel as it is very easy to double your report development time trying to make that last 10% look and feel perfect.

## Major challenges in formatting

### People Hate Scrolling Horizontally

Reading across while scrolling back and forth is difficult at best. In almost all cases, people will be happier with a longer report in order to avoid scrolling horizontally. In fact, one key formatting principle is to trade height for width.

## Browser Differences

If you are working in HTML, the big challenge is that the same exact page will look different on different browsers, versions of browsers, and machines. Colors are not uniform, fonts can vary, screen resolution differences and more can all conspire to make differences in your output. In a worst case, a page that looks fine on one browser may not show at all in another.

## Unknown and changing size of data

Perhaps the biggest challenge you will address is due to the fact that the size of your data is unknown and able to change.

Imagine you have spent much time and care using trial and error in determining the width of individual columns of a list report and feel that you have it perfect. When running a report in design mode, you generally only see the first 20 rows of data and this can be misleading. Imagine your report has 400 rows, and row # 399 has an exceptionally long value in one of the columns. Once you run your report into a "full output format like PDF or Excel, and suddenly your report does not look right ... perhaps you need to scroll right to see some of the data and one column has become exceptionally wide with large amounts of white space elsewhere.

In your report design, you then widen the offending column and believe you are ok. But, your data is changing daily and 3 weeks later an even longer value is added to the database and your formatting breaks again.

You may have the notion to run an SQL statement (or a Cognos report) to determine the width of each column in your report but you will then run into the next problem.

## Proportional and Fixed Fonts

There is a little known fact of the difference between proportional fonts and fixed fonts. This document is written using a proportional font, and using them, I will demonstrate the issue

Here are 10 X's and underneath are 10 I's in a proportional font

XXXXXXXXXX

IIIIIIIIII

The same ten characters using a Fixed Font

```
XXXXXXXXXX

IIIIIIIIII
```

Most people prefer to read proportional fonts.

As you can see with proportional fonts, the number of characters is not related to the width of display, so merely counting them is not enough. It turns out that a proportional font allows each letter to take up as much horizontal space that it needs. In reality, the width of a word, number or phrase depends on the specific combination of letters and numbers within it. So if you try to determine what the widest value in a particular column is, you will have to also take into account the font that will be used and the individual characters within the data values.

The bottom line is that determining the width of a piece of text is an art and you will never get it right.

## Wrapping

In HTML, the rule is that words cannot be broken and hyphenated. Your browser will generally only break a word when there is a space between two words or they contain a hyphen. Sometimes, you will be reporting from data where a particular value has no spaces. In this case, the browser rule is to take as much horizontal space as needed, but do not put a line break within a "word", even if your design limitations (column widths) need to be overridden. Most recently I saw some free-form text from an application where the person who created the data added an underscore between each word instead of a space. This paragraph was not "broken" by HTML or PDF and took about 2 screen widths of space and dominated the layout until discovered. (BTW: The solution was to wrap a calculation around the field replacing the underscore with an underscore AND a space so that the browser could break the line on the space.)

There are many issues in the area of formatting and layout in report development, just know that you can spend large amounts of time on a relatively small part of the report development ... the formatting and layout. If you are prone to be a perfectionist, don't let yourself be consumed by formatting.

# Some Complex Logic is Best Done in a Stored Procedure or Function

If you are a purist minded person, you may feel compelled to always solve your reporting challenges within Report Studio. This approach often leads to hugely complex reports, or reports that are very difficult to maintain or have unacceptable performance. It is easily possible to get into a situation where you have dozens of queries to solve a problem, or you have master detail reports inside of master detail reports. It is typical that you get into a hard-coding situation where you determine the number of queries that are needed even though that number may need to expand in the future.

There are other ways that you can create a report that is too complex for others to maintain.

In this situation, you should consider going partially or fully outside of Congo's for your solution.

Your options include:

1) Create one or more database views to support the report.

2) Write a stored procedure that arranges the data into a much more useful way for you to report on.

3) Create one or more functions that perform a calculation you need.

4) Have the ETL code produce a table that you report on, or that you use to simplify your report design.

5) Modify the prompt values using JavaScript when appropriate.

6) Do not use Congo's for the report but instead, write a piece of software to produce the report.

To keep yourself productive, the list above should always be in the back of your mind. Of course all come with tradeoffs, and so does using Report Studio. You will have to balance the realities of getting the external solution in place with the complexity to build your report in Report Studio and the loss of maintainability.

As other people in an organization typically create views, stored procedures etc., they take time to get completed, approved, tested and promoted and then maintenance of them is significantly slower. This part of report development is all about judgment and tradeoffs.

# Multiple Ways

One of the joys and sometimes pains of Report Studio is that there are multiple ways to create the same report or to achieve the same outcome for a part of a report.

It's a joy because you have options. If you are hitting roadblocks or coming across situations where doing it one way may create a high development burden or really bad report performance, you can throw it away and try a different approach.

On the downside, you do not know if the approach you settle on is ideal until you have spent significant time developing it, and, you will always have the nagging feeling that perhaps, did not use the right approach.

Some examples:

- You decide to use a series of queries joined together in order to produce a set of fields for a report. Alternatively you could have used "in–column filters" (calculations with logic to include/exclude data).

- You use a master-detail report to solve a problem that can be solved by using a grouped or sectioned report.

- You use a series of singletons when a master-detail may have worked better.

- You use a filter when an inner join could have performed the same result.

- You attempt to use multiple list frames to show different, but related information when a query strategy would be easier.

Which approach is right? It depends on underlying issues like size of data, actual functions used, whether or not the query runs on the Database or inside of Congo's and other factors.

Over time, you will determine which methods work best for you and come to understand the tradeoffs for each different approach, then apply them as an artist where every method has merits in a given situation.

If you follow many of the principles that I teach, you will make more right choices then wrong ones, but only deep experience will show you the right way.

# Report Must be Made from a Single Package Only*

Another core principle of Report Studio (and a limitation) is that a report can be made from a single package only. In a practical sense and at the beginner's level, this is a truth, but in a minute I'll show you a possible work around.

It is common for people new to Report Studio to want to add one field from another database that is not in the current package... Unfortunately, there is no (easy) way to do that in Report Studio. The standard and recommended solution is to have your modeler add the additional data source and model it into your package as needed and then you can add it to your report. At the beginners' level, this limitation is an absolute "no way around it" limitation.

This designed-in reality has a few important implications. Sometimes there are multiple packages that may serve your needs, each with different sets of fields available to you. You need to be really careful when selecting the package at the beginning of report development as you almost certainly will need to totally redo the report if you chose the wrong one. Also, if you do need that one more field, then it may take weeks or longer (in larger organizations) to have the field added, tested and promoted. In fact, in some industries (notably pharmaceuticals), making any changes are a large burden due the fact that everything must be carefully documented and tracked through a notorious process known as "validation".

## How to get around the one package per report limitation.

At the advanced level, there is a way around this limitation, but at a significant cost in report maintenance and a high probability of significant roadblocks. Report Studio has been designed with the intent of report developers not needing to know SQL to be able to perform their work. However, it is possible. When you add SQL to a report, you are immediately restricting the available list of developers who could fix or improve the report to those who know SQL. But sometimes, you have to do it.

In Report Studio, you can create a query from SQL and the SQL can be sent to any data source configured within Cognos. (Forgetting security constraints for this explanation).

You can add an additional field from a non-modeled table or database by using a SQL query and performing the join to you other queries in the report. As you are bypassing the model, you will have lots of housekeeping things to do like changing field names, default aggregation on numeric fields, and setting formatting options.

Keeping in mind that theory and practice are often significantly different, there are many things that could trip up your ability to do this:

- Security settings in Cognos can block your ability to use SQL at all.
- Cognos may not have a connection to the desired database.
- You may have no access to the design (names of tables and fields) of the intended database.
- A lack of a field to perform a join on.
- Database side security may block Cognoss' ability to retrieve the tables or fields you seek

If you are able to overcome all of those constraints, they you may just have a way around the "One package Per Report" limitation in Report Studio.

# Report Studio Will Not Invent Data For You

A common roadblock hit by many when beginning to build more complex reports is when the report does not show anticipated data.

> Example
> You want to show sales for each day of the week and you want to have a 7 column crosstab report with one column for each day of the week.
>
> You add day and dollar amount to your report and run it, but you see only 6 columns.
>
> Upon further investigation, you discover that the business was closed last Wednesday due to weather and no transactions occurred.
>
> What is happening is that Congos is only reporting on the data that it has... It cannot "invent" data on its' own (nor would you normally want it to). Cognos does not know what you mean to report.

This problem frequently shows up in many sneaky ways and will cause you confusion and lost time unless you are prepared to get the data another way.

## How to solve the missing data problem

Basically, to solve these types of problems, you have two choices:

1) Find the data you seek elsewhere in the package and, (with joins) produce a report showing the data you seek.
2) Invent the data and bring it into your report.

> Solving the above Example using Approach #1

Imagine you have another table that you had no intentions of including in your report... perhaps a table of web visits, and this table includes the day of the visit.
You could change your query structure around to first query the web visits table as a source to produce days you seek (assuming you have visits every day) and then join that result to your orders table (using an outer join) so that every day will be represented in the final query.

When you report on the same set of days, you will see the day when the business was closed in the report, with no value for the day. To sum up this approach, I am suggesting you can use a table totally unrelated to your reporting requirement to help you show every day in the report.

## Inventing Data for Display

You might have a situation where you need separate rows in a report where each row has a value based on different filtering conditions but one of the rows is not coming from the database (say it is some milestone reached, maybe a change due to a merger or baseline of performance) .

In this case, you can make a query containing the static data, then union it into your final query and position it accordingly. In this case, please know that in order to receive the static data row back within the query, you must have a filter on the database that uses a "real" field.... just having static data in a query will not show any results without including something from a table. In the case of a query union, you need to maintain the same number of columns and the same order, so adding a real field from the database Is really not an option (unless you happen to actually need a specific field value). However, adding a filter on a field in the database will do the trick and Report Studio will then bring back data. You may need to play around with your filter, especially if you are seeking only a single row in the union.

## Inventing a Field for Sorting or Joining

Using a calculation (data item) you can either create a value manually or calculate one based on some value in the database that will help you perform a join or allow you to force a sort order in a final query.

Often, you create a Data Item that contains a static value in multiple queries, then use that Data Item as your join field.

If you are trying to get a set of rows into a particular order, you can invent a data item which contains data, either static or calculated that will force the order as you would like. Imagine a situation where you need alphabetical, but must switch around a few rows breaking the alpha sorting (E.G. you want to show your home country first). In this case, you can add a calculation to use the regular field value, except in a few cases. In the special cases, you concoct a value that has the effect of placing the row you wish to relocate based on the normal value. In effect you switch the value to one that puts it in the right place. Then you sort on the concocted data item value instead of the actual value.

# Finding an alternative way to perform a Join

Sometimes this inventing of data is needed in a field used for joining two tables together. Imagine you have a dirty data situation where the field used for joining is corrupt, but you are being asked to produce anything, even if it is incomplete and not perfect. Imagine that you are using city information and the joins are not working on the field City ID.

Instead, you determine that zip code is a more reliable way to join the tables, even though that was not intended in the original database design. However, one database has 9 digit zip codes (postal codes) and one has 5 digit ones. In this case, you add a calculation to the table with 9 digit zip codes, removing the extra four and then use this calculated field as the join key.

Are any of these solutions ideal? No. But neither is the database from which you must work. Workarounds are part of the job, and one illustration of the huge difference between theory and practice. Most people get paid for practice so you must have these and many more tricks up your sleeve if you are to thrive in the working world.

# Conclusion

Knowing how to use a tool is merely the start of being a developer in any technology. Report Studio is no different.

In all technical solutions, there are usually underlying principles that are not well communicated, but are crucial to setting your approach to solving problems. They are hard to learn and usually you learn them in a process I call "street learning". You might get lucky and find someone that understands things at the appropriate level of abstraction, but it is rare in my experience. Finding them in books or in online postings is extremely rare.

The principles I spell out here are intended to orient you to the process of creating reports using Report Studio. The set the framework and limitations that have a significant bearing on how you will approach problems. Knowing these limitations and principles in advance, you can save much lost time and effort in not going down particular paths as you know in advance how the limitations will impact your designs.

These principles are not directly actionable, but they will color your development decisions and keep you from taking the wrong approach and do so early, before time and effort are expended.

For example, you now should understand that without knowing your data, you could make a report that is wrong and not achieve your ultimate goal of communicating to the user of your report. In a case like this, you may not even begin report development as you know what is being asked of you is not possible within the realities of the data... a 100% savings in report development time.

I have intentionally made much of this material very concise and reduced it to the simplest way of saying it. Please do not take its' length as an indication of relative importance. Some things I say in one sentence have taken me years of hands on experience to convert into a principle.

Re-read this booklet (or one section) from time to time and you will continue to gain a deeper understanding of how Report Studio wants to be used. I hope you agree that the "what you should do" is rarely taught but instead learned, and learned the hard way, and it is my sincere hope that I have brought you some of the “what you should do”.

# About the Author

Ray Hogan is a 30 year hands on diverse technologist. He has spent the bulk of his career as an applications developer working on Relational Database applications. He has learned and subsequently discarded technologies many times with the changing nature of IT.

Ray has an unusual combination of skills in that he can both do technology and teach technology. On top of his 28 years of teaching experience (karate), He spent 2, 3 year periods as a technical trainer teaching Web Development in the late 90's and then for Cognos as a Trainer in the mid 00's. As a trainer, he has a knack for simplifying complex things, providing multiple descriptions of the same thing and caring that his students succeed. As a developer, he believes that simplicity is better but simplicity is not necessarily easy. He also believes that underlying principles will help you

He currently is a VP of Business Intelligence doing hands on report development, training and software development at a Major Financial Institution in the NYC area.

He is certified in Cognos reporting, modeling and administration, and is a Certified Technical Trainer (CTT+). He has a B.S. in Electronics Engineering and is pursuing a masters in Information Systems

You can find Ray at CognosTrainers.com and on LinkedIn.

# Services and Products

## Cognos Training

We provide in class and virtual, hands-on training in all parts of Cognos. We distinguish ourselves in that our trainers have significant development experience and are excellent trainers. At the core of our trainer selection is the observation that just because a person has a technical skill, does not mean they can teach it. We use only trainers who have very significant development experience AND can explain the tools in an understandable way to people of differing technical backgrounds.

The value of a great trainer cannot be understated. Lesser trainers focus on what a feature does ... we focus on what it does for you, when to use it, alternatives and other value-creating instruction. In short, we teach you what you should do, not what you can do. We want our students to get it, to experience several "ah-has'" in our classes. We can provide training using your data. This greatly helps students understand the tools as they understand the answers they are receiving within they reports and can better grasp the cause and effect so crucial to effective training. Moreover, students leave the training much more prepared to build reports against your data. Training can be on your equipment or ours. We can provide any subset or combination of classes as you need.

Our rates are highly competitive.

Onsite or virtual. One hour or one month.

## JavaScript Report Enhancement

It is pretty common that you need Report Studio prompts to do more than they are designed to do. Enforcing data entry rules like data type, number of choices, date restrictions and more are not possible out of the box. Additionally, there are some things the Report Studio prompts cannot do like synchronizing choices between different prompts, taking a pasted list of values as a filter condition, and other higher level prompt actions. In short, you can get more out of Report Studio by using JavaScript. You can even do some report side enhancements like animated chart rotation, showing additional data in hover-overs, Ajax and more.

Finding someone with both Report Studio development experience and JavaScript programming skills is very difficult. Sure there are those who can copy and paste from Google, but often, you need even more.

If you need to enhance your prompts or reports with JavaScript, We know how to do it and have an extensive library of routines. The typical JavaScript assignment takes 4 hours or less. See our website for videos of some fairly advanced Report Studio prompt enhancements we have made.

# Consulting

Tell us how we can help you. We can act as a Sounding Board, Brainstorming, Report Troubleshooting, Build Report Conversion tools, Candidate Interviewing, extremely specific (single topic) training.... How can we help you?

# Other Booklets

Our Companion Book is "Ten Hard-to-Learn Tips for Becoming an Advanced Report Studio Developer" covers specific techniques and other things you can do to increase your development skills. Stay in touch for additional Report Studio Series booklets coming soon. We'll be announcing them on LinkedIn and through our email list.

Made in the USA
Monee, IL
04 November 2026

67384424R00022